U.S. GOVERNMENT

The Judicial Branch

Carol Parenzan Smalley

PERFECTION LEARNING®

EDITORIAL DIRECTOR   Susan C. Thies
EDITOR   Lucy Miller
DESIGN DIRECTOR   Randy Messer
BOOK DESIGN   Emily J. Greazel
COVER DESIGN   Michael Aspengren

IMAGE CREDITS

© Wally McNamee/CORBIS: p. 18; © Bettmann/CORBIS: pp. 21, 37; © Associated Press: pp. 29, 32, 35, 36, 40, 41

ClipArt.com: pp. 6, 12, 15, 34; Corel Professional Photos: pp. 4–5, 24; EEOC: p. 42; Library of Congress: p. 16; Liquid Library: back cover, front cover (main, bottom center), p. 1, 11; Perfection Learning: pp. 7, 10, 14, 27; Photos.com: pp. 33 (top, middle), 39, 43, 45; Supreme Court Curator: pp. 8, 19 (top, bottom), 20, 22, 25, 26; Supreme Court Curator: p. 9

Some images ClipArt.com, Corel Professional Photos, Library of Congress, NARA, Perfection Learning Corporation, Photos.com, Supreme Court Curator: (Chapter heading bar) pp. 3, 4, 6, 13, 17, 21, 27, 34, 44–45

A special thanks to William J. Miller, attorney, for reviewing this book

Text © 2005 by **Perfection Learning® Corporation**.
All rights reserved. No part of this book may be reproduced, stored in
a retrieval system, or transmitted in any form or by any means,
electronic, mechanical, photocopying, recording,
or otherwise, without prior permission of the publisher.
Printed in the United States of America. For information, contact

Perfection Learning® Corporation
1000 North Second Avenue, P.O. Box 500
Logan, Iowa 51546-0500.
Tel: 1-800-831-4190 • Fax: 1-800-543-2745
perfectionlearning.com

1 2 3 4 5 6 PP 09 08 07 06 05 04

ISBN 0-7891-6244-x

Contents

The Judicial Branch at a Glance 4

CHAPTER 1
Equal Justice Under Law 6

CHAPTER 2
Duties of the Supreme Court 13

CHAPTER 3
Becoming a Supreme Court Justice 17

CHAPTER 4
Behind the Scenes of the Supreme Court 21

CHAPTER 5
How the Supreme Court Works 27

CHAPTER 6
Landmark Decisions: The Court Shapes History 34

Internet Connections and Related Readings for
 the Judicial Branch 44

Glossary 46

Index 48

The Judicial Branch at a Glance

General Facts

Head of the Judicial Branch Supreme Court
Current Number of Supreme Court Justices nine
Original Number of Supreme Court Justices six
Term term of good behavior (life)
Salary (2004)
  Chief Justice $202,900
  Associate Justices $194,200
Youngest Supreme Court Justice to Serve
  Joseph Story (age 32)
Oldest Supreme Court Justice to Serve
  Oliver Wendell Holmes (retired at age 90)
Longest Supreme Court Justice Term Served
  William O. Douglas (36 years, 209 days)
First Home of Supreme Court New York City
Current Home of Supreme Court Washington, D.C.

Chapter 1

Equal Justice Under Law

These four words—equal justice under law—are carved into the main entrance of the highest court in the country, the **Supreme Court**. They reflect the goal of the Constitution to provide all citizens with equal rights under the laws of the United States. The Supreme Court is located in the nation's capital, Washington, D.C.

The Supreme Court is one of the three branches of the **federal** government known as the **judicial branch**. This branch is responsible for interpreting the Constitution of the United States. But it does not hold all the power.

U.S. Constitution, Article III

Section 1. The judicial power of the United States, shall be vested in one Supreme Court, and in such inferior courts as the Congress may from time to time ordain and establish. The judges, both of the supreme and inferior courts, shall hold their offices during good behaviour, and shall, at stated times, receive for their services, a compensation, which shall not be diminished during their continuance in office.

Section 2. The judicial power shall extend to all cases, in law and equity, arising under this Constitution, the laws of the United States, and treaties made, or which shall be made, under their authority;—to all cases affecting ambassadors, other public ministers and consuls;—to all cases of admiralty and maritime [of or relating to the sea] jurisdiction;—to controversies to which the United States shall be a party;—to controversies between two or more states;—between a state and citizens of another state;—between citizens of different states;—between citizens of the same state claiming lands under grants of different states, and between a state, or the citizens thereof, and foreign states, citizens, or subjects.

With three coequal branches of government (executive, legislative, and judicial), the federal government uses a system of checks and balances. The **executive branch** enforces the laws of the land. The **legislative branch** creates the laws. And the judicial branch focuses on cases and controversies arising from these laws and the individual rights of the nation's citizens.

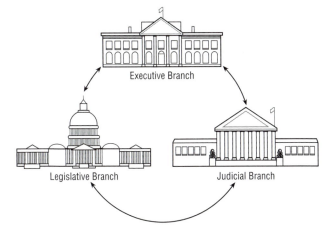

7

The Supreme Court sits at the top of the U.S. **judicial system**. Lower courts sit below the Supreme Court. The purpose of all courts is to resolve disputes. These disagreements can occur between people, organizations, individuals and organizations, and even individuals and the state in which they live.

Disputes are often resolved through trials held in a courtroom. Attorneys argue in favor of their clients. Courts try to resolve the dispute according to the laws. Some of these laws may be federal laws. Others may be state or local laws.

The Court Finds Its Footing

The U.S. Constitution established the Supreme Court in 1787. The Constitution, however, did not tell the nation's leaders how the Supreme Court should operate or what powers it should have. Because of this lack of direction, the judicial branch was not initially an equal partner in the federal government. It took time for the Court to grow into the role it plays today.

The first **bill** introduced in the United States Senate became the Judiciary Act of 1789. It divided the country into 13 judicial districts among three circuits—Eastern, Middle, and Southern. The bill called for the Supreme Court to reside in the nation's capital. The first court had a **chief justice**, or leader, and five **associate justices**.

The Court first assembled in February 1790 in the Merchants Exchange Building in New York City, which was the nation's capital at that time. The Court used its earliest gatherings to organize itself and define its processes. It wasn't until the Court's second year that it heard its first cases. The Court handed down its first **opinion** in 1792.

Merchants Exchange Building, New York City

The nine members of the U.S. Supreme Court as of 2004 are (front row, l–r) Associate Justices Antonin Scalia and John Paul Stevens, Chief Justice of the United States William H. Rehnquist, and Associate Justices Sandra Day O'Connor and Anthony M. Kennedy; (back row, l–r) Associate Justices Ruth Bader Ginsburg, David Souter, Clarence Thomas, and Stephen Breyer.

President George Washington appointed the six original **justices**. He appointed four other justices before the end of his second **term**.

Today, there are nine justices. This number has changed several times over the history of the Supreme Court. It has remained at nine since 1869, however.

Justices serve terms of "good behavior." As long as they do their job well (and want to continue working as a justice), justices remain on the **bench** for life. As of 2004, there have been only 16 chief justices and 97 associate justices. Most justices serve an average term of 15 years.

Justice Takes a Road Tour

For almost the first 100 years of the life of the Supreme Court, justices "rode circuit." They were required to hold court twice a year in each of the circuit courts. The justices did not care for this part of their job. As the country grew, touring the circuits became more difficult and more time-consuming for the justices.

The current justices still have duties related to the federal judicial circuits. However, there are other courts in the federal system that take on some of the responsibilities that the Supreme Court justices used to have. In fact, there is a whole system of courts that hears **appeals** before the Supreme Court does. These are the United States **Courts of Appeals**. These courts operate similarly to the Supreme Court, except there are 13 of these courts in different parts of the country. Most appeals in federal cases are heard for the first and last time in these courts. Not many appeals make it to the Supreme Court. Of course, parties may appeal a Court of Appeals decision to the Supreme Court and they often do. But that still doesn't mean the Supreme Court has to hear the case.

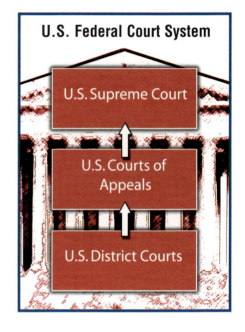

Cases reach the Courts of Appeals and the Supreme Court after they are first presented in one of the almost 100 **federal judicial districts**. A federal judicial district is a geographic area containing federal general trial

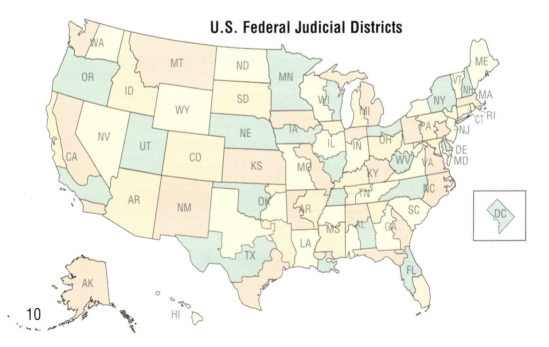

courts in the United States. There are approximately 90 districts in the 50 states. **District courts** also exist in Puerto Rico, the Virgin Islands, the District of Columbia, Guam, and the Northern Mariana Islands. Some states, such as Alaska, have one single judicial district. Others, such as California, have multiple judicial districts. There are also special-purpose federal courts, such as those that hear tax cases. More than 500 district judges hear cases in these federal courts.

Kinds of Cases

The federal court system hears approximately 300,000 cases each year. These cases are heard in the lower courts. Depending on the type of case, different laws apply.

Cases can be divided into three main categories: civil, criminal, and administrative.

A **civil case** is an action brought by a person or party to protect or preserve a civil or private right. The individual filing the suit, known as the **plaintiff**, may be seeking to recover property, to see that a contract is honored, or to protect his or her rights. The individual or organization accused of violating the plaintiff's civil or private right is the **defendant**. (Both plaintiffs and defendants are called **litigants**.) Many civil actions are settled outside of the courtroom.

A **criminal case** is brought by the government against an individual accused of a crime (the defendant). The federal judicial system only hears these cases when federal law is involved.

An **administrative case** involves rules set by one of the government agencies. There are federal laws that regulate certain business and professional behaviors. If an individual violates one of these laws, he may be called into court to defend his actions. Sometimes individuals think regulations are unfair or unreasonable. When this happens, the individual can ask a federal judge to hear the case and determine the fairness of the regulation or law.

An Eye for an Eye

The expression "an eye for an eye, a tooth for a tooth" comes from the 282 laws—known as Hammurabi's Code—carved in stone 4,000 years ago. Hammurabi was a king and chief priest of Babylonia from 1792–1750 B.C. He wrote and publicly displayed his laws for all people to understand. Violators of the Code were brought before judges. Hammurabi's laws are considered by many to be the first comprehensive legal code in history. The eight-foot-high stone on which the laws were written was unearthed in 1901–1902 by archaeologists in what is now Iraq. It is on display at the Louvre Museum in Paris, France.

Here are a few of the laws translated from Arabic:

★ If any one steal cattle or sheep . . . or a pig or a goat, if it belong to a god or to the court, the thief shall pay thirtyfold therefor; if they belonged to a freed man of the king he shall pay tenfold; if the thief has nothing with which to pay he shall be put to death.

★ If any one is committing a robbery and is caught, then he shall be put to death.

★ If a son strike his father, his hands shall be hewn off.

★ If a man put out the eye of another man, his eye shall be put out.

Duties of the Supreme Court

The Supreme Court has several duties, but the most important one is to interpret the U.S. Constitution. The Court decides if a law or action by the government violates the Constitution. This process is called **judicial review**.

When a justice is sworn into the Court, he or she takes the following oath:

> "I, [NAME], do solemnly swear (or affirm) that I will administer justice without respect to persons, and do equal right to the poor and to the rich, and that I will faithfully and impartially discharge and perform all the duties incumbent upon me as [TITLE] under the Constitution and laws of the United States. So help me God."

The (National) Court of Last Resort

The Supreme Court acts in the same way as a referee at a sporting event. It solves disputes between parties. Its decisions cannot be overruled. Only another Supreme Court ruling or an amendment to the Constitution can change a Court decision.

Thousands of cases are brought before the Court each year. The Court does not hear all of these cases. In a typical year, the Court may hear fewer than 100 cases and offer opinions on even fewer.

The Supreme Court is at the head of the federal judicial branch. It creates procedures for all federal courts to follow. The federal courts must follow the Supreme Court's decisions.

But the United States Supreme Court is not directly part of each state's judicial system. The U.S. Supreme Court only interprets state law if an issue regarding the federal Constitution is involved. It cannot make final decisions about a state's constitution.

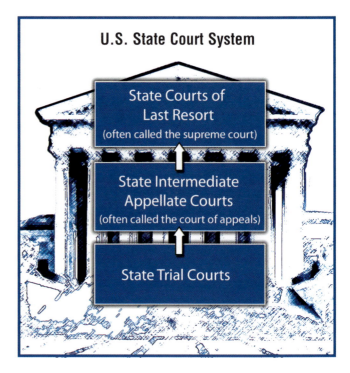

And it does not oversee state-level court procedures and operations. The Supreme Court's interpretation of federal laws can impact state-level court decisions, however. Each state has its own court of last resort to interpret state-level laws. In most states, this is called the supreme court.

Other Important Duties

Judicial review is the Supreme Court's primary duty. It does other work too. Each Supreme Court term, or session, starts on the first Monday in October. The Court meets in Washington, D.C. It no longer travels around the country to hear cases.

Each day the Court is in session, it receives an **Orders List**. Business that the Court will conduct that day is on this list. The group of cases the Court is planning to hear is called its **docket**. The Orders List also includes an ongoing list of cases that will be reviewed in the future and those that the Court has decided not to review.

In addition to hearing cases, the Court may be involved with issues involving foreign dignitaries. It can resolve maritime law disputes and consider treaties with other countries too. Sometimes the Court is called into an emergency session when there is a national crisis that requires its intervention.

The chief justice has extra duties. In addition to being the leader of the Supreme Court, he is the chairman of the Judicial Conference of the United States. He is third in line to meet with visiting dignitaries. (The president and vice president are the first two.) He delivers the annual state of the federal courts address. Oftentimes, the Supreme Court is referred to by the name of the chief justice. But perhaps one of the more enjoyable assignments is serving on the boards of the National Gallery of Art, the Smithsonian Institution, and the Hirshorn Museum.

Thankless Duty

The Supreme Court had shaky beginnings. Knowledgeable men skilled in law and national affairs did not want to accept a seat on the bench. They did not see a Supreme Court appointment as prestigious. Many thought it was a thankless job.

John Jay

John Jay was the first chief justice. He declared that the job was "intolerable." In an attempt to escape duty of the Supreme Court, Jay ran for New York governor in 1792. He lost. He tried again in 1794 and won, resigning from his position as chief justice.

Then President John Adams ordered John Marshall to be chief justice. Marshall was unsure how he felt about the assignment. But he became one of the most respected and important chief justices. He served from 1801 to 1835.

By the 1900s, an appointment to the Court was so desirable that President William H. Taft (1909–1913) preferred his new role as chief justice (1921–1930) to that of his role as president.

Today, justices are not forced to serve on the Supreme Court. And Taft's path to the Court from the White House is a rare occurrence. How are Supreme Court justices appointed?

John Marshall

William H. Taft

Chapter 3

Becoming a Supreme Court Justice

Who can become a Supreme Court justice? You might be surprised to learn that you do not need to be an attorney to become a justice. You also do not have to attend law school to become a justice.

There are no official qualifications for justices. In the history of the Supreme Court, all the justices have had training in the law, however. Most justices were involved in legal and political careers before their time on the Court. Several justices were trained in federal and state government positions. They were members of Congress, governors, cabinet appointees, and even U.S. president!

Presidential Appointment

The president appoints U.S. Supreme Court justices. The Senate must approve them. If the president appoints a justice who does not have a legal background, the Senate may not approve the appointment.

Approval by the Senate begins with a confirmation process. The Senate Judiciary Committee investigates the president's choice for justice. The Committee requests a report about the candidate's legal background from the American Bar Association. The American Bar Association monitors attorney action around the country.

Hearings are held. The Committee questions the nominee and witnesses, people who speak about the character and experiences of the nominee. After the hearings, the Committee decides whether to recommend the candidate to the full Senate for a vote.

The hearing process is not always easy for the nominee. The nominee's views, character, and personal history are examined. When President Ronald Reagan nominated Judge Robert Bork to the Court, Committee members were not kind to Bork. They thought Bork's views were radical. The Senate did not approve his appointment. Today, when judicial nominees are severely criticized and not appointed, they are said to be **borked**.

Robert Bork

U.S. Supreme Court Justices

For a full listing of every Supreme Court justice, including information about what state they came from, who appointed them, and what years they served, visit **www.supremecourtus.gov/about/members.pdf**.

Removed by Impeachment

Supreme Court justices hold their appointments for life. They cannot be removed for their decisions or opinions. They can, however, be removed if they commit a high crime or misdemeanor.

To be removed from the Court, they must first be charged by the U.S. House of Representatives. The Senate then holds court. The justice must be convicted in the Senate trial by a two-thirds majority vote.

No justice has ever been removed from the Court through **impeachment**. But one came close.

In 1805, the House of Representatives charged Justice Samuel Chase. The House claimed that Chase conducted himself improperly in making political remarks while "riding circuit." But when the impeachment proceedings moved to the Senate, other political issues distracted them. The Senate did not have the two-thirds majority vote needed to impeach Chase. He remained a Supreme Court justice until 1811, when he died.

The House has charged no other justices. But others, when faced with political pressure or failing health, have chosen to resign.

Samuel Chase

Supreme Court Firsts

The faces of the Supreme Court have changed throughout the Court's history.

In 1916, Louis Brandeis was appointed to the Court as its first Jewish justice. Anti-Semites often attacked his opinions. (An anti-Semite is someone who has negative feelings toward Jewish people.) One of the justices on the Court was so opposed to Brandeis's appointment that he refused to sit next to him in session. Brandeis believed in the rights of the individual. He also supported freedom of speech. He retired from the Court in 1939 as one of the Court's greatest justices.

In 1967, the U.S. Supreme Court welcomed its first African American justice. President Lyndon B. Johnson appointed Thurgood Marshall, the grandson of a slave. Marshall often argued for the rights of African Americans. His first appearance at the U.S. Supreme Court was not as a justice, but as an attorney presenting a case. Marshall won 29 of the 32 cases he argued before the Court. He retired from the Supreme Court in 1991 at age 82.

Thurgood Marshall

Sandra Day O'Connor became the first female Supreme Court justice in 1982. President Ronald Reagan appointed her. He promised that women would serve in high positions during his presidency. O'Connor was the right woman at the right time to fill an open seat on the Court. She has often been the deciding vote in decisions. As a child, O'Connor grew up on a cattle ranch. She thought she wanted to be a cattle rancher. Her grandmother encouraged her to look at other career options while she was growing up. "There should be no barrier for any of you to decide which direction you want to go and which path to follow," says O'Connor.

Sandra Day O'Connor

Chapter 4

Behind the Scenes of the Supreme Court

There are only nine justices on the Supreme Court, but more than 18 hands to do the work. Let's meet a few of the 400 people behind the scenes at the Supreme Court.

Personal Assistants: Law Clerks

Each justice can have four assistants, or law **clerks**. Clerks are law school graduates. Some clerks have previous experience working in federal courts. Law clerks perform legal work that the justices do not have time to do. They research. They read **petitions** put before the Court. And they summarize their findings for the justices. Sometimes justices rely on their law clerks for advice!

The first woman law clerk, Lucille Lomen, at her desk. She clerked for Associate Justice William O. Douglas from 1944–1945.

Law clerks work for one-year terms. But other Supreme Court employees stay for longer periods. These long-term employees help to run the day-to-day operations of the Supreme Court.

The Officers of the Court

Two key people in the Supreme Court office are the Court's attorneys. They are known as the **Legal Office**. They handle the Court's legal concerns.

The clerk spearheads daily operations of the Court. This office handles all paperwork, scheduling, and record keeping. Before attorneys can present before the Supreme Court, they must be admitted to the Supreme Court bar. The clerk processes thousands of applications each year for admittance.

Security is a concern at the Supreme Court. Over two hundred security officers work in the building and on the grounds. The person who manages this security force is the marshal. The marshal is also the official timekeeper in the Court. He or she uses red and white lights to signal lawyers as they speak.

The director of data systems manages the Court's computers and information technology system.

The chief justice has an administrative assistant. He or she keeps the chief justice on schedule and organizes his workload.

All Court opinions and decisions are recorded. This is the responsibility of the reporter of decisions. The reporter must follow a special format. The decisions are published in the *United States Reports*.

Members of the press (such newspapers, magazines, and Internet sites) rely on the public information officer to provide information on Court actions.

The Court has its own library. The librarian manages its more than 500,000 volumes. The court curator handles other important historical documents.

All of these employees work inside the Supreme Court building.

Supreme Court Building

"The Republic endures and this is the symbol of its faith."
—Chief Justice Charles Evans Hughes, 1932, while laying the cornerstone of the Supreme Court building

The Supreme Court did not always have a building to call its own. It wasn't until 1932 that construction began on the Court's current home in Washington, D.C. The Court first met in the Merchants Exchange Building in New York City. When the nation's capital moved to Philadelphia, the Court moved into Independence Hall. Later it met in City Hall, also in Philadelphia. Once in Washington, D.C., Congress lent the Court space in the Capitol Building until a building for the Court was constructed.

Architect Cass Gilbert designed the Supreme Court building. He envisioned a structure as impressive as the government branch buildings. The building's foundation measures 385 feet by 304 feet. It extends four stories high. Gilbert did not live to see the final construction of the building. His son finished the project in 1935.

There are sixteen marble columns at the main west entrance. They support the portico. Here the words "Equal Justice Under Law" are inscribed.

Above this motto are nine figures sculpted by Robert Aitken. These figures represent important people involved in the creation of the building.

On either side of the main entrance are two marble figures by sculptor James Earle Fraser. On the left is a female figure, *Contemplation of Justice*.

On the right is a male figure, *Guardian or Authority of Law*.

This sculpture of Moses and the Ten Commandments sits on the east side of the U.S Supreme Court building.

Entering the Building

Visitors to the Supreme Court building enter through a set of bronze doors on the west side of the building. The doors are 17 feet high, 9 ½ feet wide, and weigh 13 tons. Each door holds relief panels showing significant events in the evolution of justice in the western world.

There are also important figures on the east entrance to the building. Sculptor Hermon A. MacNeil created a group of marble figures representing great lawgivers—Moses, Confucius, and Solon—and *Means of Enforcing the Law*, *Tempering Justice with Mercy*, *Settlement of Disputes Between States*, *Maritime*, and other functions of the Supreme Court. The words "Justice, the Guardian of Liberty" are part of the sculpture.

Beyond the entrance is the Great Hall. Busts of all chief justices who have served on the Court rest on marble pedestals along the walls.

The Court Chamber lies at the east end of the Great Hall. The justices meet in the Chamber. It is 82 feet by 91 feet. The ceiling is 44 feet high. There are 24 marble columns inside the Chamber. The justices sit on a raised mahogany bench during sessions.

There are many other rooms and offices throughout the Supreme Court building. Each justice and his or her law clerks have their own spaces. There are a library and conference rooms as well.

Tour the Building

You don't have to travel to Washington, D.C., to see the Supreme Court building. Visit **www.oyez.org**, click on the "Tour" tab, and begin a virtual tour of the building that houses the highest court in the country.

Chapter 5

How the Supreme Court Works

"The Honorable, the Chief Justice and the Associate Justices of the Supreme Court of the United States. **Oyez***! Oyez! Oyez! All persons having business before the Honorable, the Supreme Court of the United States, are admonished to draw near and give their attention, for the Court is now sitting. God Save the United States and this Honorable Court!"*

These are the words announced by the Court's marshal as the justices file into the Chamber. The justices enter the courtroom through three entrances behind the bench. They are seated by **seniority**, with the chief justice and the two most senior justices in the center. The least senior of the justices sits on the far right of the bench.

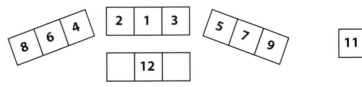

The Supreme Court of the United States
Courtroom Seating Chart

1. Chief Justice Rehnquist
2. Justice Stevens
3. Justice O'Connor
4. Justice Scalia
5. Justice Kennedy
6. Justice Souter
7. Justice Thomas
8. Justice Ginsburg
9. Justice Breyer
10. Clerk of the Court
11. Marshal of the Court
12. Counsel

Reaching the High Court

Thousands of petitions are submitted to the Court each year for consideration. About 100 are actually heard before the Court.

Cases heard by the United States Supreme Court concern the interpretation of the U.S. Constitution or federal law. At one time in the history of the Supreme Court, all cases brought before it were heard. Today, law clerks help to sort through the petitions seeking a **writ of certiorari** (or cert). This order from the Court asks the lower courts to send the case records. Law clerks summarize the facts, analyze legal issues, and make recommendations to the Court about which cases it should hear. The justices then decide if the case is worth hearing. In order for a specific case to be heard, it must be chosen by at least four of the justices. When the Court does not select a case or **grant cert**, the ruling of the lower court stands.

Clarence Earl Gideon

Experienced attorneys file many petitions before the Court. However, ordinary citizens who believe they have been denied justice in a lower court file petitions too. Sometimes convicted criminals submit their own petitions. These petitions are sometimes called **pauper petitions**. Most of these are rejected, but not all.

Clarence Earl Gideon filed a petition from his Florida jail cell. He wrote it in pencil on prison stationery. Gideon had been convicted of breaking and entering. He could not afford an attorney when he was arrested. He requested a court-appointed attorney and was denied. He defended himself in court and lost. In his petition to the Supreme Court, he claimed that without an attorney to defend him, he had been denied a fair trial. The Court agreed with him and overturned his conviction. Today, because of Gideon's pauper petition, criminal defendants are guaranteed legal representation.

You can view Gideon's original petition to the United States Supreme Court at **dpa.state.ky.us/library/advocate/mar03/gidpetition.html**.

Before presenting to the Court, attorneys for each side of the case present a **legal brief**. This is a written legal argument. It states each party's viewpoint. It presents the case and its facts. Justices read these briefs before hearing the **oral argument**.

Speaking Before the Court

Attorneys presenting cases are seated at the tables facing the bench. When arguing the case, each attorney steps up to a lectern before the chief justice. There are two lights on the lectern. When the attorney sees a white light, he has five minutes left to present his case. When he sees the red light, he must stop his presentation. One hour is usually allowed for both sides to present their arguments before the Court.

After hearing the case, the justices discuss it privately. They take a preliminary vote. A justice representing the **majority opinion** in the case will then write a first draft of the decision for the other justices to read. Oftentimes, the chief justice selects the justice who will write the opinion. He may even select himself to author the opinion if he is in the majority vote. Justices who agree with the majority opinion but do not agree with the reasoning of the majority may write a **concurring opinion**. Justices who do not agree with the majority may write a **dissenting opinion**.

What makes a majority?

A majority is one more than half. Since the U.S. Supreme Court is currently made up of nine justices, at least five justices have to agree about an issue for it to be the majority opinion.

U.S. Solicitor General Theodore Olson argues before the U.S Supreme Court on September 8, 2003.

Before announcing the decision to the arguing attorneys and the public, all justices review the final opinion for approval. The public information officer releases the opinion after the justices complete their review.

One Attorney's Experience: Arguing Before the Court

Iowa-based attorney Richard Doyle argued before the U.S. Supreme Court in 1987. He shares his experience:

Please tell us about the case you presented before the Supreme Court.

Our client, a passenger in a small French-built airplane, was injured when the plane crashed shortly after takeoff from an airfield in rural Iowa. Our client filed a lawsuit in state court seeking recovery of his damages. The lawsuit against the French manufacturer claimed the crash was caused by a design defect in the airplane. The case was transferred to the United States District Court. Under the Federal Rules of Civil Procedure, we requested that the French manufacturer produce its engineering and design drawings and flight test data concerning the airplane.

Did the manufacturer share its records?

The manufacturer refused to produce its records. It claimed the federal rules did not apply, and that under the terms of a treaty signed by the United States, France, and other countries from around the world, the manufacturer was not required to produce the requested records. The main issue before the Supreme Court was whether the treaty was the exclusive and mandatory procedure for obtaining documents and information from a foreign national that was a party to the litigation. The Supreme Court held that the treaty did not deprive the district court from ordering the French manufacturer to produce the records requested under the Federal Rules of Civil Procedure.

What was the path your case took to reach the United States Supreme Court?

The products liability suit, alleging the French-built plane was defectively designed, was filed in Iowa state court, the state where the crash occurred. Under federal rules, the lawsuit was transferred to federal court at the request of the French company. A dispute between the parties arose when the French manufacturer refused to produce certain records. The federal district court judge ordered the French company to produce the records. The French company appealed the ruling to the Eighth Circuit Court of Appeals (the next level in the federal court system). The Eighth Circuit agreed with the district court's ruling. The French company then appealed the decision to the United States Supreme Court (the highest court in the Federal court system).

What skills helped you prepare to present before the Supreme Court?

I had a keen interest in researching, solving problems, and reading.

Were you afraid or anxious when you presented?

I was not afraid, but I was naturally anxious before my argument to the highest court in this country. Once I stood up, any nervousness or anxiousness evaporated as I concentrated on my argument and answering questions from the justices. This would not have been possible without my extensive preparation, which included practicing my argument in front of other lawyers.

What did you learn as an attorney and as a person through the experience of presenting to the United States Supreme Court?

No matter how daunting the task may first appear to be, success is possible. Proper preparation is the key. I knew the facts of the case and the applicable law better than anyone in the courtroom that day. That inspired my confidence.

Was there an event in your childhood that persuaded you to enter the legal profession?

I became fascinated with the law when I took a business law course in high school. I decided then that I wanted to go to law school.

After high school, what education was required for you to practice law? Do you still go to school?

I earned an undergraduate degree (4 years of college) and a law degree (3 years of law school). Iowa requires every lawyer to attend at least 15 hours of continuing legal education each year. Those hours are usually obtained through attending legal education courses at seminars and conventions. Most states have a similar continuing legal education requirement.

What would you recommend to a reader who might want to follow in your footsteps and practice law?

Learn to love to read and search for your own answers to questions. Participate in your school's mock trial, speech and debate, and music and drama programs. These activities will help you become more at ease in speaking before public groups, such as juries and courts. Participate in school clubs, student government, and community service organizations. A lawyer active in the community is a better lawyer and a better person. Study hard. Good grades are essential for admission to law school.

To read the Court's ruling on Attorney Richard Doyle's case, visit **caselaw.lp.findlaw.com/scripts/getcase.pl?navby=case&court=us&vol=482&page=522**.

The Court's Year

The Court meets from the first Monday of October until June. Some days are reserved for hearing cases. Other days are used for reading petitions or writing decisions. Opinions for cases heard during this time are usually released before the Court breaks in June.

Sometimes special sessions must be called. In July 1974, the Court gathered to hear a special case. The country's president, Richard Nixon, was in trouble. Audiotapes of conversations recorded by President Nixon in the Oval Office were requested. Nixon believed he did not have to share these tapes. He claimed "executive privilege." President Nixon believed he had the right to withhold this information to preserve confidential communications and secure national interest. Sixteen days after hearing the arguments in U.S. v. Nixon, the Court decided that the president must release the tapes. Nixon did as the Court asked and then resigned.

President Richard Nixon gestures toward written accounts of conversations he had in the White House while announcing he will turn them over to House impeachment investigators and the public.

High Traditions

The Court has changed during its more than 200-year-old history. Many of its traditions, however, have remained the same.

The Court seats itself by seniority. The chief sits in the center. His senior-most associate is to his right. The next senior sits to his left.

Members of the Court wear black robes.

In its earliest day, the Court wrote its opinions with quill pens. While computers have replaced the quills for writing, white quill pens are still placed at each counsel or attorney's table when the Court is in session.

Before beginning a session, the Court performs a "conference handshake." Each of the nine justices shakes hands with the others.

The seal of the Supreme Court is used on official Court documents. It shows a single star beneath a set of eagle's claws, representing the creation of "one Supreme Court."

Chapter 6

Landmark Decisions
The Court Shapes History

In its 200-year history, the Supreme Court has heard and decided many cases. Many of its decisions affect our daily lives. Here are a few Court decisions that have changed the course of American history.

Dred Scott v. Sandford

Year: 1856

Question Before the Court: Was Dred Scott a free man or a slave?

Case: Dred Scott was a slave in Missouri. He asked the state of Missouri to free him and his wife from slavery because he had traveled with his master to "free territories." The Missouri courts ruled that only people born into slavery were slaves. Scott claimed that his residence in a free territory made him a free man. But the Missouri Supreme Court disagreed. Scott remained a slave.

Decision: The United States Supreme Court upheld the decision of the Missouri Supreme Court. The Court decided that slaves were property and not citizens with rights. Scott remained a slave.

Dred Scott

Korematsu v. United States

Year: 1944

Question Before the Court: Did President Franklin D. Roosevelt and Congress function beyond their war powers when they restricted the rights of Japanese Americans during World War II?

Case: Under Presidential Executive Order 9066 and congressional statutes, Japanese Americans were excluded from areas considered critical to national defense and potentially vulnerable to espionage. One Japanese American, Toyosaburo "Fred" Korematsu, violated Civilian Exclusion Order No. 34 of the U.S. Army by remaining in San Leandro, California.

Decision: The Court sided with the government. It believed that the need to protect against espionage carried more weight than Korematsu's individual rights.

President William J. Clinton (right) presents Toyosaburo "Fred" Korematsu with a Presidential Medal of Freedom at the White House in 1998.

Brown v. Board of Education of Topeka

Year: 1954

Question Before the Court: Does race segregation of children in public schools deprive minority children of equal protection under the laws as guaranteed by the 14th Amendment?

Case: African American children were denied admission to public schools that were attended by white children. The law had permitted segregation according to race. This legalized separation was known as Jim Crow, and it required "colored" people to use different public schools, restaurants, and public restrooms. The resources at the white and black schools (such as the buildings, classes offered, and teacher salaries) were nearly equal.

Decision: The Court rejected the law that suggested that separate facilities were permissible as long as they were equal. Separate but equal was considered unconstitutional when it came to public education.

> **Fourteenth Amendment, Section 1**
>
> All persons born or naturalized in the United States, and subject to the jurisdiction thereof, are citizens of the United States and of the state wherein they reside. No state shall make or enforce any law, which shall abridge the privileges or immunities of citizens of the United States; nor shall any state deprive any person of life, liberty, or property, without due process of law; nor deny to any person within its jurisdiction the equal protection of the laws.

A group of students in Atlanta, Georgia, gather around a radio to hear the announcement that the U.S. Supreme Court has ruled segregation in public schools unconstitutional.

Changing Opinion in Changing Times

Plessy v. Ferguson

In 1896, a gentleman named Plessy challenged a Louisiana law that required "coloreds" to ride in "equal but separate" railroad cars. Plessy was light-skinned, but he had an African American grandparent. He was legally "colored."

The Court ruled in favor of keeping the "separate but equal" law by eight to one. The dissenting justice—John Marshall Harlan—said that the "Constitution is color-blind."

For the next 60 years, African Americans were treated unequally under Jim Crow. The Court finally rejected the doctrine when it considered Brown v. Board of Education. This time the Court had a different interpretation of the U.S. Constitution.

Who Was Jim Crow?

Jim Crow was not a person, but a way of life for African Americans during the 1800s through the mid-1950s. The words became a racial slur meaning "black," "colored," or "Negro." Acts of racial discrimination toward blacks were often referred to as Jim Crow laws and practices. For example, the railcar for "coloreds" was called the Jim Crow car.

Learn more about this time in America's history by visiting The History of Jim Crow at **www.jimcrowhistory.org/home.htm**.

Miranda v. State of Arizona

Year: 1966

Question Before the Court: Is the Fifth Amendment violated if police question individuals without first explaining their right to an attorney and their protection against self-incrimination?

Case: The Court heard several similar cases where individuals were held in custody or deprived of their freedom. Police officers, detectives, and prosecuting attorneys questioned them without first telling them their rights under the Constitution.

Decision: The Court determined that prosecutors could not use statements made by suspects when their rights were not explained to them before questioning. Today, police must a give warning to suspects, explaining the right to remain silent and the right to have an attorney present when questioned.

The Miranda Warning

You have the right to remain silent. Anything you say can and will be used against you in a court of law. You have the right to speak to an attorney, and to have an attorney present during any questioning. If you cannot afford an attorney, one will be provided for you at government expense.

The Fifth Amendment

No person shall be held to answer for a capital, or otherwise infamous crime, unless on a presentment or indictment of a Grand Jury, except in cases arising in the land or naval forces, or in the Militia, when in actual service in time of War or public danger; nor shall any person be subject for the same offence to be twice put in jeopardy of life or limb; nor shall be compelled in any criminal case to be a witness against himself, nor be deprived of life, liberty, or property, without due process of law; nor shall private property be taken for public use, without just compensation.

Tinker v. Des Moines Independent Community School District

Year: 1969

Question Before the Court: Does prohibiting the wearing of armbands in public school—as a form of symbolic protest—violate the First Amendment's freedom of speech protection?

Case: Three Des Moines school students decided to protest the Vietnam War by wearing black armbands to school. School officials asked the students to remove the bands or face suspension. The students refused and were suspended.

Decision: The Court ruled that the First Amendment protected the right to wear armbands. The Court believed that the school officials lacked justification for imposing the limitation of the bands. They failed to show that that the wearing of the bands would interfere with an appropriate school environment.

The First Amendment

Congress shall make no law respecting an establishment of religion, or prohibiting the free exercise thereof; or abridging the freedom of speech, or of the press; or the right of the people peaceably to assemble, and to petition the government for a redress of grievances.

Do School Dress Codes Limit Freedom of Speech?

Does your school have a dress code? Do you think it limits your ability to express yourself? Divide your class into two groups. One group is in favor of dress codes. The other group opposes dress codes. Research the topic of dress codes and First Amendment rights. Then hold a debate.

Regents of the University of California v. Bakke

Date: 1978

Question Before the Court: Did the University of California's Medical School violate both the Fourteenth Amendment's equal protection clause and the Civil Rights Act of 1964 when it applied an affirmative action policy that resulted in the rejection of Bakke's application repeatedly?

Case: Even though Allan Bakke had higher grades and test scores than some of the successful minority applicants applying for a position at the medical school, he was repeatedly refused admission. Bakke argued that he was a victim of racial discrimination and was not selected because he was white. The college claimed that it reserved a set number of spaces in each class for minority students to reverse long-standing discrimination against minority races.

Allan Bakke is followed by reporters on his first day of medical school in 1978.

Decision: No single majority opinion was reached in this case. The Court did not find in favor of Bakke. It ordered the school to admit him, however. The Court concluded that admission selection based on race was permissible.

Listen to the two sides present their case before the Court at **www.oyez.org/oyez/resource/case/324/audioresources**.

Upholding the Decision 25 Years Later

In 2003, Barbara Grutter applied to University of Michigan Law School. As a white woman with high grades and test scores, she was denied admission. Like Bakke, she took her case before the Supreme Court. She lost. The Court determined that the law school had the right to deny her admission. The school had the right to create a diverse student body and to consider many admissions factors, including race.

Barbara Grutter (left) talks with reporters on April 1, 2003, while the U.S. Supreme Court considers her case.

Civil Rights Act of 1964

Title I

Barred unequal application of voter registration requirements, but did not abolish literacy tests sometimes used to disqualify African Americans and poor white voters.

Title II

Outlawed discrimination in hotels, motels, restaurants, theaters, and all other public accommodations engaged in interstate commerce; exempted private clubs without defining "private," thereby allowing a loophole.

Title III

Encouraged the desegregation of public schools and authorized the U.S. Attorney General to file suits to force desegregation, but did not authorize busing as a means to overcome segregation based on residence.

Title IV

Authorized but did not require withdrawal of federal funds from programs that practiced discrimination.

Title V

Outlawed discrimination in employment in any business exceeding 25 people and created an Equal Employment Opportunity Commission to review complaints, although it lacked meaningful enforcement powers.

United States v. Eichman

Date: 1990

Question Before the Court: Did the Flag Protection Act violate freedom of expression as protected by the First Amendment?

Case: In 1989, the Supreme Court decided in Texas v. Johnson that the Texas law making flag burning illegal was unconstitutional. Then Congress passed the Flag Protection Act because it disagreed with the Supreme Court's decision in Texas v. Johnson. The Act made it a crime to destroy an American flag or any likeness of an American flag that was "commonly displayed." Several prosecutions resulted from the Act.

Decision: The Court overturned the law. It felt that it limited an individual's right to free expression.

Flag Protection Act (1989)

(a)(1) Whoever knowingly mutilates, defaces, physically defiles, burns, maintains on the floor or ground, or tramples upon any flag of the United States shall be fined under this title or imprisoned for not more than one year, or both.

(2) This subsection does not prohibit any conduct consisting of the disposal of a flag when it has become worn or soiled.

(b) As used in this section, the term "flag of the United States" means any flag of the United States, or any part thereof, made of any substance, of any size, in a form that is commonly displayed.

The Court is rich in tradition and history. Each year the Supreme Court hears new cases and makes decisions based on its current interpretation of the Constitution. These new cases will shape the future of this country.

Internet Connections and Related Readings
for the Judicial Branch

www.supremecourtus.gov

Find out what's on the Court's docket, learn when the Court will hear what cases, read opinions handed down by the Court, and read the rules of the Court.

www.usscplus.com/info

Read about the Court's history, traditions, procedures, justices, and building.

www.supremecourthistory.org

Learn about the history of the Court, how the Court works, and how best to research the Court. Also includes biographies on many of the justices who have served on the bench.

bensguide.gpo.gov

Enter Ben's Guide to U.S. Government for Kids and explore the branches of government and other interesting topics that relate to the U.S. government.

www.oyez.org/oyez/frontpage

See what's happened at the Supreme Court on any day in history, read about all of the justices who have served on the Court, take a virtual tour of the Supreme Court building, and read summaries of some of the Court's most famous cases.

Thurgood Marshall by Lisa Aldred. A biography of one of the great American Supreme Court justices. Perfection Learning, 1990. [RL 7 IL 5–10] (4351101 PB) (4351102 CC)

The Supreme Court by Patricia Ryon Quiri. A history and description of the Supreme Court of the United States, explaining its origins in the Constitutional Convention, its early history, and some landmark cases. Children's Press, 1998. [RL 3.8 IL 3–5] (6878206 CC)

The letters *RL* in the brackets indicate the reading level of the book listed. *IL* indicates the approximate interest level. Perfection Learning's catalog numbers are included for your ordering convenience. *PB* indicates soft cover and *CC* indicates Cover Craft.

Glossary

administrative case (ad MIN uh stray tiv kays)   case involving a violation of rules set by a government agency

appeal (uh PEEL)   request to take a lower court's decision to a higher court for review

associate justice (uh SOH shee uht JUS tis)   member of the Supreme Court who is not the chief justice

bench (bench)   seat where a justice sits in the courtroom; also used to describe a court in general

bill (*bill*)   idea for a law that is being considered by the legislative branch of the government

borked (borkt)   term for when a judicial nominee is severely criticized and not approved by the Senate; refers to the denial of Judge Robert Bork's appointment to the Supreme Court

chief justice (cheef JUS tis)   lead justice of the Supreme Court

civil case (SIV uhl kays)   action brought by a person or party to protect or preserve a civil or private right

clerk (klerk)   law school graduate who assists a justice by reading, writing, and researching issues before the Court

concurring opinion (kon KUR ing oh PIN yuhn)   opinion that agrees with the majority opinion (see separate glossary entry) but does not agree with the reasoning used to form the opinion

Courts of Appeals (korts uhv uh PEELS)   courts between the district courts and the U.S. Supreme Court that hear cases on appeal only

criminal case (KRIM uh nuhl kays)   case brought by the government against an individual accused of a crime

defendant (dee FEN duhnt)   individual or organization accused of violating a civil or private right in a civil case or of committing a crime in a criminal case

dissenting opinion (di SENT ing oh PIN yuhn)   opinion that disagrees with the majority opinion (see separate glossary entry)

district court (DIS trikt kort)   federal court that is part of a geographical district

docket (DOK et)   group of cases the Court is planning to hear

executive branch (ig ZEK you tiv branch)   part of the government that enforces the laws of the country

federal (FED uh ruhl)   of or relating to the U.S. government

federal judicial district (FED uh ruhl jyou DISH uhl DIS trikt) geographic area containing federal general trial courts

grant cert (grant sert) act of choosing a case to be heard

impeachment (im PEECH muhnt) act of charging a government official with wrongdoing and possibly removing him or her from office

judicial branch (jyou DISH uhl branch) part of the government that interprets laws and the Constitution

judicial review (jyou DISH uhl ree VYOO) process by which the Court decides if a law or action by the government violates the Constitution

judicial system (jyou DISH uhl SIS tuhm) U.S. court system

justice (JUS tis) member of the Supreme Court

legal brief (LEEG uhl breef) written legal argument

Legal Office (LEEG uhl AW fis) office of two attorneys who handle the Court's legal concerns

legislative branch (LEJ uhs lay tiv branch) part of the government that writes and passes laws

litigants (LIT uh guhnts) plaintiffs and defendants

majority opinion (muh JOR uh tee oh PIN yuhn) opinion held by the greatest number of justices

opinion (oh PIN yuhn) decision made by the Court

oral argument (OR uhl AR gyou muhnt) verbal argument made by an attorney before the Court

Orders List (OR duhrs list) business that the Court will conduct on a given day

oyez (OH yez) Latin for "hear ye"

pauper petition (PAW puhr puh TISH uhn) petition filed by a citizen who cannot afford legal counsel

petition (puh TISH uhn) written request for the Court to hear a case

plaintiff (PLAYN tif) individual or organization making a complaint in a lawsuit

seniority (seen YOR uh tee) ordered according to years of experience, from most experienced to least experienced

Supreme Court (suh PREEM kort) the highest court in the United States

term (*term*) length of time one person serves in office *or* the length of time the Court meets each year

writ of certiorari (rit uhv ser shee uh RAIR ree) order from the Court requesting a lower court to send the files of a case they have decided to hear

Index

Adams, John, 16
administrative case, 11, 46
Aitken, Robert, 24
American Bar Association, 17
Bork, Robert, 18
Brandeis, Louis, 19
Brown v. Board of Education of Topeka, 36, 37
Chase, Samuel, 19
City Hall, 23
civil case, 11, 46
Civil Rights Act of 1964, 40, 42
clerk, 21–22, 26, 28, 46
criminal case, 11, 38, 46
dissenting opinion, 29, 46
district court, 10–11, 30, 46
Douglas, William O., 4, 21
Dred Scott v. Sandford, 34
equal justice under law, 6, 24
federal judicial district, 10–11, 47
Fifth Amendment, 38
First Amendment, 39, 43
Flag Protection Act (1989), 43
Fourteenth Amendment, 36, 40
Fraser, James Earle, 24
Gideon, Clarence Earl, 28
Gilbert, Cass, 23
grant cert, 28, 47
Grutter, Barbara, 41
Hammurabi's Code, 12
Holmes, Oliver Wendell, 4
Hughes, Charles Evans, 23
impeachment, 18–19, 47
Independence Hall, 23
Jay, John, 15
Jim Crow, 36–37
Johnson, Lyndon B., 19

judicial review, 13, 14, 47
judicial system, 8, 11, 14, 47
Judiciary Act of 1789, 8
Korematsu v. United States, 35
legal brief, 29, 47
Legal Office, 22, 47
MacNeil, Hermon A., 25
majority opinion, 29, 47
Marshall, John, 16
Marshall, Thurgood, 19
Merchants Exchange Building, 8, 23
Miranda v. State of Arizona, 38
Miranda warning, 38
Nixon, Richard, 32
O'Connor, Sandra Day, 9, 20
opinion, 8, 13, 18, 19, 23, 29–30, 32, 33, 47
oral argument, 29, 47
Orders List, 14, 47
pauper petitions, 28, 47
petitions, 21, 28, 32, 47
Plessy v. Ferguson, 37
Reagan, Ronald, 18, 20
Regents of the University of California v. Bakke, 40–41
Senate Judiciary Committee, 17
Taft, William H., 16
term, 4, 9, 22, 47
Texas v. Johnson, 43
Tinker v. Des Moines Independent School District, 39
U.S. Constitution, 6–7, 8, 13–14, 28, 36, 38, 39, 43
United States v. Eichman, 43
Washington, George, 9
writ of certiorari, 28, 47